A PORTRAIT OF
BATH

JOHN CLEARE

HALSGROVE

First published in Great Britain in 2004

British Library Cataloguing-in-Publication Data
A CIP record for this title is available from the British Library

ISBN 1 84114 374 X

HALSGROVE
Halsgrove House
Lower Moor Way
Tiverton, Devon EX16 6SS
Tel: 01884 243242
Fax: 01884 243325
email: sales@halsgrove.com
website: www.halsgrove.com

Printed and bound by D'Auria Industrie Grafiche Spa, Italy

CONTENTS

DEDICATION

To the architects, the builders and their patrons of past centuries whose talents, skills and enterprise created the city we admire today.

INTRODUCTION

Of all the gay Places the World can afford,
By Gentle and Simple for Pastime ador'd,
Fine Balls, and fine Concerts, fine Buildings, and Springs,
Fine Walks, and fine views, and a Thousand fine Things...
Not to mention the sweet Situation and Air,
What Place, my dear Mother, with Bath can compare?

Christopher Anstey, The New Bath Guide *1767*

Bath is a city of hills. Or to be more precise, the ancient city centre stands in a bend of the River Avon hemmed in by steep hillsides. Over the centuries the city has crept upwards so that most Bathonians – and there are around 80,000 of them – have a hill to climb when they go home.

Northwards rise the Cotswolds from which the eponymous National Trail descends Lansdown Hill to finish at the Abbey, plumb in the city centre. To the south, a spur of Somerset's Mendip Hills forms equally high ground. Several tributary valleys join the Avon hereabouts and at Bath the Roman Fosse Way crossed the river on its way from Exeter to Lincoln: it is obvious from its topography why the city still awaits a proper bypass. Any interested and active visitor to Bath should first take an overview of the city from one of the surrounding heights from where its context is well seen.

While the geography of Bath may be interesting, its history is fascinating. The Roman Baths which gave their name to the city are internationally famous, but the origin of the settlement goes back, by tradition, far earlier. A Prince Bladud, expelled from court as a leper, became a swineherd. Noticing that his pigs were curing a prevalent skin disease by wallowing in warm mud pools nearby, he followed their example and recovered. He returned to court, eventually became king, and founded a settlement on the site of the therapeutic hot springs – and incidentally fathered Shakespeare's King Lear.

Some 900 years later the invading Romans, familiar with such things, built elaborate baths on the site beside a temple dedicated to Sulis, the Celtic Goddess of Wisdom and Healing, with whom they identified their own goddess, Minerva. The settlement became the spa of *Aquae Sulis*, with its obvious derivation of *Hat Bathu* first recorded in 676.

Bathu became an important Anglo Saxon monastic centre and Edgar, first king of all England, was crowned here in 973. Domesday Book records Bath as the largest town in Somerset, and after its revolt against King William Rufus and subsequent devastation, it rapidly recovered to flourish as a centre for the medieval wool trade.

In 1499, work started on the present fine Abbey, designed in restrained Perpendicular style, which continued for some three hundred years. Meanwhile the hot springs, though Crown property, were administered by the ecclesiastical authorities and were frequented by, among others, Anne of Denmark, wife of James I. Nevertheless, records suggest that the surrounding town was a pretty seamy place, and the hygiene at the hot springs left much to be desired.

It was the arrival of the dandy 'Beau' Nash in 1702 which really put Bath on the map. With his appointment as the city's 'Master of Ceremonies,' Bath soon became synonymous with good taste, high fashion and an elegant lifestyle. Society flocked to the spa to take – and drink – the curative waters. Celebrated throughout Europe, this was Bath's Golden Age, and wealthy entrepreneurs moved in to develop what was then still essentially a medieval town.

Various civic buildings appeared; the original Pump Room and Assembly Rooms were built and in 1777, an imposing Guildhall. But perhaps more notable was the almost explosive residential development of which Ralph Allen was the patron and the two John Woods, father and son, the most prolific architects. Starting in 1729 and throughout the following half century, the Woods and others built a series of dignified squares and parades, terraces and crescents using the locally quarried, honey-coloured Bath stone.

The mastery of perspective and proportion, of position and vista by these architects and builders is still awesome, and their creations are classical, the epitome of all that was best of the Georgian legacy. By stark contrast, the modern visitor will be shocked by the appallingly-ugly post-war redevelopment of the badly-bombed southern end of the city centre.

Expansion continued throughout the following century, and while Bath remained fashionable and boasts many fine Victorian buildings and facilities, the city gradually faded from its pre-eminence. The Industrial Revolution had happened and in 1810, to considerable local consternation, the canal had arrived linking London to the great mercantile port of Bristol just 10 miles down river. And then the railway came, bringing with it commercial development and some industry. By the early twentieth century, Bath's claim to fame was as a genteel 'health resort for invalids in winter.'

My own first memory of Bath dates to what must have been 1939, when I was just three years old. We stayed with my godmother in her spacious flat which I've since located as a handsome Victorian villa in Sydney Buildings. I vividly recall that I was forbidden, for obvious reasons, to venture into the garden which ran down to the by then long-disused canal. We had travelled down from London on the Great Western Railway and what a great railway it was; the Box Tunnel, clouds of steam, polished brass and chocolate and cream livery. In my mind Bath will always have strong ties to both the GWR and the Kennet and Avon canal.

My next visit came some years later when on a day off school we sneaked away on our bikes and rode down to Bath to visit the cinema, safe as we thought, from vigilant school masters. It proved a round trip of almost 60 miles so I guess we earned our forbidden fruit. We visited the Roman Baths too that day, though I don't recall being very impressed.

An elderly citizen, born and bred in the city, recently confided to me one reason for Bath's renaissance over the past half century. 'Before the War,' he explained, 'the place was staid and stagnant, populated essentially by masters and servants. There was no dynamic middle class. Then came 1940, the Admiralty took over the town lock, stock and barrel and thousands of young Naval personnel and civilian staff were drafted down from London. Every spare room was requisitioned for billets at a guinea (£1.05) a week. Suddenly there was a middle class in the town, things started to happen and we never looked back.'

Modern Bath, while still dignified, surprisingly green and leafy, is certainly vibrant once again. It was declared a World Heritage site by UNESCO in 1987. The shops are excellent, attracting visitors from miles around. There is a busy university with an active student population and the city has dozens of elegant restaurants, bistros and bars. An International Music Festival, an orchestra, concerts, the Theatre Royal, the Victoria Art Gallery and several important museums maintain Bath's strong cultural tradition.

The Royal Victoria Park is a favourite venue for hot air balloonists, Bath Rugby Club is famous in the sport, and regular meetings take place at the Race Course high on Lansdown Hill, while the now fully-restored canal and the River Avon are thronged with recreational traffic. The downside is serious traffic congestion and – so residents will tell you – excessive, albeit lucrative, tourism.

Unfortunately, the lovely glowing Bath stone, an oolitic limestone, is soft and prone to weathering and pollution damage. Frequent chips and gashes in pillar and portico bear witness to the 1942 Blitz by Nazi bombers, and by the mid-twentieth century, with money scarce and utility the norm, many of the beautiful buildings had become neglected, run down and partitioned into flats.

Exploring Bath on foot, as I have been doing for this book, nosing into streets, mews and alleys not normally seen by visitors, and casting my eyes up and down and around as photographers do, it is evident that despite considerable renovation, this situation still pertains in many places. Much remains to be repaired, renovated, secured or sympathetically replaced if our great grandchildren are to enjoy this small, inspiring and still stunningly-handsome city.

John Cleare, July, 2004

Very early on a summer morning is the time to admire the geometry of Bath from a hot-air balloon. This view from an altitude of about 1000 feet encompasses many of the city's most memorable features. On the far left stands the Victoria obelisk with Marlborough Buildings and the Royal Crescent close by and Kelston Round Hill on the horizon. High Common rises beyond the Crescent with Lansdown Crescent to its right where Beckford's Arch is clearly visible and Beckford's Tower just discernible on the skyline. St Stephen's Tower is seen further to the right while Camden Crescent stands beside the far right margin. The magnificent Circus occupies pride of place in the foreground.

VISTAS & VIEWPOINTS

Clustered in its narrow valley and spreading up the surrounding hillsides, the intricate street patterns of Bath are well seen from several viewpoints on the surrounding high ground. Probably the best is in the vicinity of Sham Castle, the apparently-imposing Georgian folly near the golf club house on the lip of Bathampton Down. This lies on the excellent Bath Skyline Walk, opened by the National Trust, which traverses most of the hill crest south east of the city. Other good and relatively uncluttered viewpoints are Camden Crescent and the lip of Beechen Cliff in and around Alexandra Park.

The Abbey tower dominates this early morning view over the city from North Road on the slopes of Bathampton Down.

Opposite: The stately north-facing façade of Prior Park is illuminated by the summer evening sun in this view over leafy Bathwick and Widcombe from Camden Crescent.

The view to the north west from Sham Castle: Camden Crescent is well seen above Hedgemead Park
with the tree-clump summit of Kelston Round Hill (218m/715 ft) on the left skyline.

From Beechen Cliff, the Royal Terrace is seen in context with High Common beyond.

This panorama looks north from Alexandra Park. The railway station and nearby modern developments are seen at the bottom of the picture, the Abbey, St John the Evangelist Catholic Church and 'The Rec' rugby ground lie beyond, and in the distance, Royal Crescent with Beckford's Tower on the skyline.

A pattern of roofs and terraces cloaks the slopes of Beacon Hill in this view to the north-north-west from just below Sham Castle.

The morning sun picks out the distinctive tower
of St Stephen's Church on Lansdown Road, a
landmark in many views over the city.

The distinctive tower of St Stephen's Parish Church stands at the junction of steep Lansdown and Richmond Roads. Built in 1840, the church was not consecrated for a further forty-nine years, until the altar had been properly aligned.

Hill-top Sham Castle was commissioned by the entrepreneur Ralph Allen to improve the view from his home on North Parade.

An early jogger stretches beside Sham Castle – now seen to be indeed a 'sham'.

PROSPECTS & CURIOSITIES

There are many reminders of the denizens of Bath – the patrons, developers, philanthropists and eccentrics – who have peopled the city over the years. Inscriptions, armorial bearings and the names of streets, squares, buildings and parks recall past glories, extinct peerages and the forenames of wives, mistresses and numerous progeny. Everywhere in and around the city the observant pedestrian will find pleasing prospects and interesting architecture and notice fascinating cameos and intriguing details, bringing the past to life and explaining much of the present.

Spring sky over the classical façade
of Marlborough Buildings.

There is a friendly feeling about the jumbled backs of these houses in the vicinity of St James's Square.

The view down steep Bathwick Hill on the south eastern side of the city.

Opposite: A handsome façade on Bathwick Hill, little changed over nearly two centuries.

In this view from High Common, evening light catches the clustered backs of Marlborough Buildings.

Interesting patterns formed by the backs of Marlborough Buildings overlooking Royal Victoria Park.

A steep perspective in Park Street on a summer evening.

These steps lead up to the once-handsome terrace of Walcot Parade overlooking busy London Street.

View towards the corner of Rivers Street
and Julian Road from the terraced pavement
of Brunswick Place. What was the
'Old Red House. Rivers Street Branch'
proclaimed on the corner wall?

These colourful buildings have somehow survived later and smarter developments on George Street.

Above: Stern-visaged Walcot Chapel (1815) on London Street.

Left: In this view from Cleveland Bridge, the gardens and yards around Walcot Chapel on London Street back onto the river.

This Edwardian avenue, continuing the Bath tradition of classic terraces, is one of several above Beechen Cliff adjoining Alexandra Park. All bear the names of celebrated men of letters.

Another dying year in the derelict cemetery of St John's, Bathwick on
the corner of Henrietta Road and Bathwick Street.

Details.   *Above:* Cavendish Road.

Right: Park Place.

Details.   *Left:* Brock Street.

Opposite: Grove Street: the date above the window labels its developer as a creationist. In 1650, Bishop Ussher of Armagh had calculated the creation of the world at 4004 BC, thus this date equates to AD 1788.

The Great White Queen presides over the entrance to the Victoria Art Gallery in the Guildhall building. The inscription reads: 'H.I.M. Victoria. Erected in Loyalty and Love by the women of Bath 1901'.

Opposite: The Guildhall, built in 1777, was enlarged in 1893. The Cupola (above) and the classically-themed frieze (below).

Detail on the elaborate Victorian corner
of George and Milsom Streets.
The arms are those of Bath.

Right: John Ellis's striking Dispensary Building stands at the northern end of Cleveland Bridge. The inscription reads: 'In Memorial of John Ellis, Esq., formerly of Southwark and for many years a resident in Bath. To whose persevering labours and munificent benefactions this Dispensary mainly owed its erection and pecuniary support. He died Oct 31st 1856 aged 86. Erected July 1857.'

Below: Would John Ellis have approved of the décor on this modern conveyance parked outside his Dispensary?

Seen on Upper Borough Walls in the old city centre.

Traffic-clogged Cleveland Bridge, built in 1827, was another Henry Goodridge design. The Earl of Cleveland was another patron of Bath developments.

Victorian – and modern – decoration on the Midland Road river bridge.

Trompe l'oeil on the corner of Grove and Argyle Streets. The faded panel reads: 'The George Gregory Book Store Lending Library. 1 Bridge (?) Street. Well Stocked with all the Latest Fiction'

The arms of William Pulteney, First Earl of Bath, crown the impressive central mansion in Great Pulteney Street. This long, dignified avenue, unfortunately now a busy through road, was built for the Earl in 1789 by Thomas Baldwin, and both Jane Austen and William Wilberforce were sometime residents.

Bath boasts two of the rare 'New Standard Letter Boxes' designed by J.W. Penfold in 1887, both on Great Pulteney Street.

Spring time amid the smart villas on Cleveland Walk.

Detail on the Great Western Railway
viaduct by the river bank.

CRESCENTS & CIRCUSES

These classic, formal buildings were largely the work of the architect John Wood, a Yorkshireman who settled in Bath in 1727, and his son, also John, with their patrons the Duke of Chandos and Ralph Allen, a rich local magnate and owner of the stone quarries on Combe Down. Their most famous creation was the ostentatious Royal Crescent, built in 1767 by the younger Wood, its majestic sweep containing, behind 114 huge Ionic columns, no fewer than 30 houses, several now hotels or museums. The grassy slopes between the Crescent and Royal Avenue are today a favourite venue for Bathonians to picnic and relax. Camden Crescent, almost vernacular by comparison, was built a few years earlier.

Pages 48–51: The Royal Crescent.

The eastern extremity of the Crescent
– like the bows of a great battleship.

Opposite: Even the lamp post echoes the
atmosphere of the Royal Crescent.
Marlborough Buildings are seen beyond.

How the iron-shod carriage wheels must have rumbled on these cobbles.

Opposite: The stately residence at the western extremity of the Crescent.

Seen in its entirety on a summer evening, the Royal Crescent is certainly an extraordinary building.

Facing the morning sun, Camden Crescent looks out over the city.

This shapely bow-front with verandah neatly rounds off the southern end of Camden Crescent.

LANSDOWN CRESCENT

Many consider Lansdown Crescent, built in 1789 by John Palmer, the most attractive of the formal terraces. Approached by a long steep hill it is probably the most rarely viewed by visitors.

Among the more intriguing former denizens of Bath was the eccentric and reclusive multi-millionaire William Beckford, who purchased Number 20 Lansdown Crescent in 1822, having sold his home, Fonthill Abbey, some 25 miles away in Wiltshire. The Abbey, a fantastic gothic folly which collapsed in 1825, is today his main claim to fame. Beckford proceeded to buy the houses to left and right. He joined the former, actually across a mews lane in Lansdown Place West, with a distinctive connecting arch designed by the-then fashionable young architect Henry Goodridge. The latter he used as a library and as 'sound-proofing' from his neighbours. He then acquired a mile long strip of undeveloped land leading from the Crescent to the summit of Lansdown Hill itself where Goodridge built him an Italianate tower – another fantasy project completed in 1827. The approach strip he had landscaped with avenues, grottos and a tunnel. Apart of course from Lansdown Crescent itself, all that is left today is the Tower, owned by the Bath Preservation Trust as a museum of Beckfordiana.

Lansdown Crescent, above its steep meadow, has a distinctly rural flavour.

Above: The Crescent sweeps round gracefully to the southeast.

Left: Lansdown Place West and Beckford's Arch.

Beckford's Arch.

Beckford's Tower rises over his massive tomb (above) on the crest of Lansdown Hill.

Beckford's incredible Fonthill Abbey
– an artist's impression from an old engraving.

The appropriately majestic central properties of the Crescent.

This elegant bow-front completes the Crescent
at its south-eastern extremity.

Well-worn pavement as Lansdown Place West
steepens towards Somerset Place.

Lansdown Crescent and the tower of St Stephen's provide a symmetrical backdrop to the extensive acres of High Common where young golfers stand by a tee. Medieval ridge and furrow is still evident in low light and hay was harvested here within living memory.

THE CIRCUS

The Circus, completed in 1754, was the masterpiece of John Wood the Elder. It consists of 99 houses set in three equal arcs around a circular 'square' in the centre of which grow five, now huge, plane trees. Doric, Corinthian and Ionic columns are all represented, while beautiful, highly detailed, friezes complete the decoration, the upper one under the cornice properly visible only in low summer light. Clive of India, Thomas Gainsborough and David Livingstone were among its famous residents.

Afternoon light on the northern-most of the three segments of The Circus.

Georgian grandeur – the corner
with Bennett Street.

Detail of the charming cherubic upper frieze that encircles the Circus below the cornice.

Stone acorns mount guard along
the impressive balustrade.

The Circus also sports a lower frieze, a pelmet almost, of intriguing detail.

THE BATHS & THE ABBEY

Although significant Roman artifacts had been unearthed throughout the eighteenth century, it was not until a century later that workmen discovered the Roman Baths themselves, and the site was properly excavated in 1880. The Great Bath, originally under a vaulted roof, was the centre of an elaborate system of baths and temples. Still lined with its Roman lead, it is some five feet deep and fed by natural hot springs at a steady 120 degrees F (49C) through the original plumbing. The stone piers, pavements and lower walls are Roman, the columns, the terrace above and the adjoining Pump Room complex, late Victorian, although the handsome Pump Room itself is a 1796 Georgian classic.

Opposite: The classical Victorian façade of the Roman Baths
building on the Abbey Churchyard.

Above and opposite: The Roman Baths.

THE ABBEY

Bishop Oliver King began the building of the present Abbey in 1499 after a dream in which he saw angels climbing ladders up to heaven. In due course, his vision was immortalised in stone on the magnificent West Front. There were many restorations between 1603 and the 1960s, the former after serious damage during the Dissolution of the Monasteries in the 1530s, the latter after Second World War bombing. Besides the West Front, the abbey is famed for its flying buttresses and superb fan vaulting.

Early morning sun lights the Abbey in this view from near Sham Castle.

Above and opposite: The stone-flagged Abbey Churchyard is flanked
by the Roman Baths building, cafés and shops.

Towering 49m/162 ft against the sun, the Abbey is seen from the strangely-named
Orange Grove below its north-eastern corner.

Pages 83–85: The magnificent West Front sports Bishop King's famous ladders to heaven, with God seated in His Glory high above.

Inscribed 'Water is Best. Bath Temperance
Association 1861', this little statue stands
beside the Abbey at the foot of High Street.
Unfortunately, the girl's pitcher seems to have spilt.

DOWNTOWN BATH

The busy shopping streets in the heart of Bath agreeably incorporate both pre- and post-Georgian buildings. Sally Lunn's house dates to 1482 but has Roman, Saxon and medieval foundations. Milsom Street, lined with many of the more important shops, was architect-designed in 1762. By contrast, a group of hideous post-war developments house chain stores, offices and car parks in the Southgate, Corn Street and Broad Quay area near the river at the southern end of the city centre. Most of the pre-Georgian or later, less-formal, buildings, lie in the quaint, narrow lanes or alleys off the main streets, and today typically house boutiques, cafés and small specialist shops. An excellent Farmers' Market operates in the old Victorian Midland Road railway station. As a varied and comprehensive shopping centre, compact enough to be explored on foot, Bath has much to recommend it.

Smart shops line Milsom Street.

Shoppers in Burton Street with Milsom Street beyond.

Above: On George Street.

Opposite: A pavement flower seller on Union Street.

Quaint Northumberland Place links
Union Street and High Street.

Saville Row beside the famous Georgian Assembly Rooms is a narrow lane with several antique shops.

Left: Looking towards Alfred Street up the narrow alley of Bartlett Street.

Opposite: Bartlett Street continues steeply down to George Street – this area is known for its antique shops.

This fine Georgian building stands at the bottom of Milsom
Street between the pedestrian thoroughfares of Burton Street
(left) and Old Bond Street.

Right: Sally Lunn's House in narrow Lilliput Lane dates to 1482 and is home not only to the indulgent Sally Lunn bun, invented in 1680, but also to a kitchen museum.

Overleaf: The arms of Caroline of Brunswick, Queen to George IV, dignify this stately pharmacy in Argyle Street.

A GREEN CITY

From the surrounding hills, Bath is incredibly green – it seems almost a forested city. Thanks probably to the way it was developed, and by whom, it certainly has a profusion of mature trees, shrub-filled gardens and tree-rich open spaces. Among them, Royal Victoria Park is the largest, containing the Botanic Gardens and various curiosities; it links up to the garden-lined Royal Avenue and the grassy sward below Royal Crescent. On the river bank near the Abbey, the attractive Parade Gardens were originally created by Ralph Allen and leased to the council for the use of Bath ratepayers who may use them without charge. Visitors must pay a nominal entrance fee. Across the river, Sydney Gardens lie astride the Kennet and Avon Canal. Inspired by London's Vauxhall Pleasure Gardens, they were laid out in 1794 by Thomas Baldwin and described at the time as 'the most spacious and beautiful Public Garden in the kingdom', but the various small feature buildings are Edwardian reconstructions of the originals. Alexandra Park is more suburban, but its hill top situation perched on the lip of wooded Beechen Cliff makes it a rewarding viewpoint.

Left and opposite: The Victoria obelisk on Royal Avenue marks the formal entrance to Royal Victoria Park. The inscription reads: 'Her Majesty Queen Victoria married to his Royal Highness Prince Albert of Saxe Coburg Gotha February 10th 1840'.

The Park Keeper's Cottage beyond the obelisk. The inscription on this side reads: 'The Inhabitants and Visitors of Bath to the Princess Victoria on the attainment of her majority 24 May 1837'. And lower down, more tragically: 'Prince Consort Albert the Good, born 1819 died 1861 aged 42'.

Spring flowers on Royal Avenue.

The glory that was never Greece
– a Victorian urn beside Royal Avenue.

This Sphinx broods over a pedestrian gateway onto Royal Avenue.

Left: Among various *objets* in the Botanic Gardens is the Rev. Essington's Sundial.

Below: This imposing tree, a *Populus lasiocarpa* (Salicaceae) imported from China, was planted in 1900.

Right: The 'Temple of Minerva' dates to the 1924 Empire Exhibition at Wembley, where it was part of Bath's exhibit and was rebuilt here two years later.

Below: In the deep shadows of Great Dell lurks this monolithic bust of Jupiter by John Osborn, 1879.

Sydney Gardens: the gable end of the reconstructed 'Greek Temple'…

... while beyond the flowers, Sydney Place stands across the road.

Left, below and opposite: The Parade Gardens rise from the banks of the Avon and the Abbey towers beyond.

Schoolboys play cricket on a summer evening on North Parade
Cricket Ground, the home of Bath Cricket Club. The spire of
the Roman Catholic church of St John the Evangelist
(1863) rises in the distance across the river.

A calm summer evening: Bath is a favourite venue for hot-air ballooning.

PRIOR PARK

Ralph Allen (1694 – 1764) was a local entrepreneur who made a fortune revolutionising the postal service. A notable philanthropist and patron of much of Bath's development, he acquired a steep combe on the hillside above the city's southern outskirts and there, over the thirty years until his death, he developed a dramatic landscape garden. The valley was landscaped by 'Capability' Brown, the Wilderness was schemed by Alexander Pope, and an exotic Palladian Bridge – one of only four in existence anywhere – was designed probably by one of the Woods, who were Palladian aficionados. Overlooking the head of the combe, the striking mansion had been completed by the elder John Wood in 1748. Over the ensuing two centuries, however, the gardens became almost forgotten, falling into neglect then decay while the mansion itself became an important Roman Catholic boarding school. Eventually rediscovered, the gardens were gifted to the National Trust in 1993 and, with restoration to their original layout still on-going, are open to the public

In this view of the Palladian Bridge over the third lake, Prior Park mansion rises over the head of the combe.

The mansion is seen beyond the Sham Bridge feature.

Opposite top: This is the classic view down the combe towards the Palladian Bridge,
the three lakes, and distant Walcot and Beacon Hill.

Opposite below: Graffito on the Palladian Bridge.

BATH UNIVERSITY

Specialising in technology, Bath University traces its origins back to the Bristol Trade School of 1856. Building on Claverton Down, high over the city adjoining Bathampton Down, was begun in 1964 and a Royal Charter was granted in 1966. The campus stands in a broad landscaped park, from where a city park and ride scheme also operates.

The University campus – southern aspect.

The Parade is the focal point of the campus.

Flower-filled container-beds prettify this view looking across the eastern end of the
Parade towards the Department of Electronic and Electrical Engineering.

RIVER
&
CANAL

THE RIVER

Rising in the southern Cotswolds, the Avon makes a tight bend at Bath before flowing a further dozen or so miles to the tide at Bristol. Though several weirs control once frequent flooding, the riverside area round the 'Rec' – the Rugby Ground opposite the city centre – is still known as Bog Island. A Sustrans cycleway follows the Avon towpath to the western outskirts of the city where it joins an abandoned railway and continues on to Bristol. Tourist boats ply the river upstream and downstream from the Riverside Walk by Pulteney Bridge, and from the Boating Station upstream from Cleveland Bridge. Pulteney Bridge itself, inspired by Florence's Ponte Vecchio, was designed by Robert Adam in 1770 and lined with little shops. It is one of Bath's most celebrated sights, and an attractive riverside walk links it to North Parade Bridge. The west bank is dominated by The Empire, a towering edifice fronting the Orange Grove, built in 1899 as a hotel but now converted to private apartments, with the ground floor given over to restaurants and bars. As the Royal Navy HQ in the Second World War, it served as the operations centre for the Battle of the Atlantic.

It is no surprise that the river complicates the road system, and for through-traffic from north or south the only by-pass to Cleveland Bridge is via narrow lanes leading to the anachronistic if quaint Avon toll bridge at Bathampton.

The Empire dominates this view of the Avon, Parade Gardens, Pulteney Bridge and the Weir from the Riverside Walk.

A spring afternoon on the Riverside Walk. The Empire, the Guildhall dome and
the spire of St Michael with St Paul are seen left of Pulteney Bridge.

The Avon towpath below Green Park Road and downstream from the railway station
is almost sylvan and is the first section of the cycleway to Bristol.

Above and opposite: Bathampton Bridge spans the Avon with the Toll House at its northern end.

THE KENNET AND AVON CANAL

Linking the Thames at Reading to the Severn tideway at Bristol with a man-made cut of 57 miles between the Kennet and the Avon, the canal was opened in 1810. Built by John Rennie, it was a fine engineering achievement, rising over 450 feet with 105 locks and crossing the gorge-like Avon valley on two impressive aqueducts as it approached Bath. Its arrival caused mayhem in snooty Bath, with the residents of the Sydney Gardens area insisting on the ornate embellishment of the local bridges and canal buildings to dispel any taint of commercialism. Cleveland House, actually built over the canal on Sydney Bridge, was the canal company headquarters. The final 65 foot/20m descent to the Avon was through the Widcombe Flight of six locks below the attractive back-gardens of Sydney Buildings and Abbey View Gardens. Commercially successful until bought out by the railway, by the 1950s the canal had fallen to complete dereliction, but its attempted closure by the government was strongly resisted, money was raised, the canal restored and eventually reopened to navigation in 1990. Once again there is a permanent lock keeper at Widcombe, and a steady succession of boats and barges, now recreational rather than commercial, passes up and down the old K & A.

A narrow-boat passes under decorative Sydney Bridge.

An autumnal view from Bathwick Bridge, a favourite section of the towpath for Bathonians.

Locking down through the Widcombe flight in autumn, Sydney Buildings beyond.

A similar view in summer just below Pulteney Gardens Bridge.

Pages133–135: Bath displays its nautical traditions, in the colours of spring (right) and autumn (overleaf).

Bathwick Marina.

Widcombe Chapel, above the final locks,
is noted for the tract on its roof.

Above and overleaf: Cleveland House stands astride the canal on Sydney Bridge.
An autumn view…

...no less atmospheric in spring.

Above: This magnificent chimney belonged to the long-gone pump house at Widcombe Locks.

Left: One of the two ornamental cast-iron footbridges in Sydney Gardens.

The canal at Bathampton, a timeless scene little changed over a century.
The George Inn, on the right, was the setting for of the last duel to be fought in England.

Canalside cottages at Bathampton.

Above: A narrow boat crosses the Dundas Aqueduct into Brassknocker Basin
below Monkton Combe on its way towards Bath.

Overleaf: Colourful narrow boats moored against the towpath.